The Ten Domains
of Effective Goal Setting

Build Wealth with Common Stocks

Hire Train Monitor Motivate

The Ten Domains of Effective Goal Setting

Achieve Your Dreams in the Essential Areas of Life

David J. Waldron

Country View

Country View
https://davidjwaldron.com
Carlisle, Pennslyvania USA

Printed and distributed by Kindle Direct Publishing,
an Amazon.com company.
21 16   2 1 2 3

Print ISBN: 978-0692605752
eBook ASIN: B01A1G1IGM

Cover design by Stacie White at Cover Design Studio

DEDICATION

For Suzan. You are my inspiration.

CONTENTS ▌

CONTENTS

S everal years ago, I had the privilege of attending an out-standing self-improvement seminar in New York, titled the *Master's Course*. My favorite takeaway from the workshop was a goal setting exercise based on a holistic approach to achieving excellence in one's life.

The template uses ten domains—or categorized essential areas of life—at both the personal and professional levels. It changed my life or at least my approach to mapping it.

To this day, it drives my goal setting, both short and long term, supporting my effort in producing many personal and professional outcomes for which I am proud as much as humbled. I have yet to find a simpler, more productive approach toward making the most of what is important to me; and caring for those who are dear to me.

One of my primary goals in life is to make a living by making a difference in the lives of others. Thus, my motivation for sharing this timeless treasure for a structured approach to goal setting in the pursuit of excellence in one's personal or professional life.

The Ten Domains of Effective Goal Setting presents in three parts.

Part I: Set Achievable Goals explores the importance of ascribing to three basic rules of goal setting; and imparts how to replace a subconscious attempt at achieving our dreams with a more conscious, counterintuitive approach that increases the chances for success.

Part II: The Ten Domains, presents how each area embodies an essential component of a well-rounded life.

The Ten Domains:

1. Spirituality
2. Family
3. Health
4. Education
5. Career
6. Money
7. Social
8. Leisure
9. Community
10. Projects

By separating a life's journey into the Ten Domains, we create opportunities for discovering ways to improve our lives at the personal and professional levels, both in the near term and further down the road. This approach is designed to create a more balanced and hopeful existence.

Part III: Achieve Your Dreams attempts to pull it all together to ensure each reader has completed a goal setting plan designed for success. Since not every goal comes true or presents as intended, Part III also addresses the importance of losing and winning with grace and dignity.

The Ten Domains may be trimmed, expanded, or rewritten with more relevant alternatives based on one's values and core beliefs. And each may be moved up and down the numbered list to reflect personal and professional priorities.

My intention is to offer the generic aspects deemed essential for a typical life within today's complex society. The domains are listed in the original order presented to me as I have yet to find objection to the priority of the ranking or to the broad definition of each domain.

Nevertheless, any goal setting strategy should be fun, creative, and attainable. Pursuing stretch goals, or hard to reach dreams, are essential for ensuring we are not taking ourselves off the hook; although reaching our intended outcomes is what is most important. That is why I recommend throughout the book, a prerequisite of setting goals that you are confident in achieving. Pursue perceived, achievable goals; complemented by expansive, and thereby more challenging ambitions.

My sincere hope is this simple yet powerful goal setting template, *The Ten Domains of Effective Goal Setting,* supports your quest to achieve the personal and professional dreams that are relevant to your life's journey, today and tomorrow; next week and next month; this year and next; five and ten years from now; and forever and always.

David J. Waldron, Author

PART I

SET ACHIEVABLE GOALS

When not achieved as intended, a goal is just that, a goal. Whether an aspiration, ambition, dream, target, purpose, or objective—whatever you want to call a goal—it is perhaps one of the most exhilarating as well as frustrating occurrences in life. Achieving a goal may be the most rewarding of moments. On the contrary, failing to reach a dream is one of life's more disheartening personal or professional experiences.

That is why it is crucial to set what are believed to be attainable goals, thus giving you an increased opportunity for joy; and, at the same time, leveraging against unwanted disappointment.

That said, genuine goals are indeed challenging. But the relative level of difficulty in achieving a goal is what makes it worth setting in the first place. "I hope to wake up tomorrow," for most individuals is not a goal but a simple reality.

For someone with a chronic illness or life-threatening injury, it may be an accomplishment without prior equal.

Therefore, it is important for each reader to determine what is special to him or her. What is the game changer? The elusive, although attainable dream? The simple accomplishment? The purpose in one's life?

Goals are one-way private contracts that determine the perceived value of our existence, often providing a measurement of our self-worth. Thus, it is imperative to keep things in perspective and not allow failure to define us nor success to spoil us. Goals are meant to keep us moving forward in this sometimes crazy thing called life. Nonetheless, never allow a failure—or an achievement for that matter—to become more important than life itself. Be humble in defeat as well as in victory.

* * *

Effective goal setting requires three general rules of the thumb that encompass planning, simplicity, and structure.

One

Have a Plan and Work the Plan

Regardless of the level of difficulty, or the personal importance of a dream, the acts of setting and achieving our goals happen more often if we write them down. For that reason, it forever remains the first rule of goal setting.

Rule #1: Write your goals down.

Goals that are written have a higher chance of actual achievement. I am of the belief that goal setting is about having a plan and working the plan. As life sometimes goes, the blueprint may not work as intended, although by having a written plan and working it with rigor, something good may happen when you least expect it.

Whether you choose a traditional paper notebook; smartphone or tablet notes app; or desktop word processing software, write your goals down in a simple yet clear and concise manner. It is a contract between you and yourself. Hence, treat it as such by signing and dating your plan. Rewrite and edit, as necessary, until you are comfortable with the language and format. But write it down, read it often, and revise it whenever necessary or practical. Life changes; therefore, the written plan that guides it needs to as well.

Two

Give Your Plan a K.I.S.S.

The key to making the Ten Domains approach to goal setting both believable and sustainable is to develop objectives within each domain for both short and long term ambitions. It is crucial to keep your plan succinct, and that brings us to the second rule of thumb for effective goal setting.

Rule #2: Keep It Super Simple (K.I.S.S.)

As a fervent believer in the K.I.S.S. concept—or the keep it super simple approach to life—I update each domain at the beginning of the year by setting at least one annual goal, e.g., this calendar year, and at least one objective that stretches beyond the year. I then, on occasion, visit the list to monitor progress, making adjustments as warranted by life's fluid and ever-changing landscape.

And yes, sometimes unexpected vicissitudes are distressing. But tragedy and heartbreak aside, remember these words of wisdom:

" *The pain of change is long forgotten when the* "
benefits of the change are realized.

Change is inevitable, and one may argue the only consistent event we may count on in life. Thus, a critical component of any goal setting exercise is the willingness to make necessary adjustments along the way.

Regardless of any change, and the resulting discomfort, keep your goals super simple. Your chances of attaining each may multiply accordingly.

Three

Use S.M.A.R.T Goals

It may seem a redundant cliché, although using a well-worn acronym in goal setting could be the difference between success and failure in reaching your desired outcomes. And it is therefore included as the third rule of goal setting within the Ten Domains.

Rule #3: Be S.M.A.R.T. in your goal setting.

Front test your written goals using George T. Doran's S.M.A.R.T. approach: *specific, measurable, attainable, realistic,* and *time-bound;*[1] inspired by Peter Drucker's legendary management by objectives concept.[2]

Doran suggests we be specific when writing down our goals; ensure our ambitions are measurable; set only goals we believe are achievable; be honest in our self-assessment by committing to targets that are realistic and relevant given the resources available to us; and establish time-specific deadlines to reach our objectives. For example:

> As an avid learner, I will read at least one book each
> month, during the hours I set aside in my personal
> calendar. Then, upon completion, write a brief narra-
> tive in my online diary of how each book entertained
> me (fiction) or enlightened me (nonfiction.)

The above illustrative goal is specific in its clear objective of reading a minimum of one book each month; measured by recording the results in personal calendars and diaries; attainable by allowing an entire month for reading at least one book amid a busy schedule; realistic in the sense the goal setter knows oneself as a passionate reader; and time bound in that he or she chooses and records specific timelines.

The S.M.A.R.T approach to goal setting is imperative for achieving dreams that are practical and achievable. Remember to integrate the S.M.A.R.T. concept into each of your written goals.

* * *

[1] George T. Doran, "There's a S.M.A.R.T. Way to Write Management's Goals and Objectives," *Management Review,* American Management Association Forum, 1981. 35-36

[2] Peter F. Drucker, *The Practice of Management* (New York: Harper & Brothers, 1954.)

Four

Be→Have→Do

I hope readers do not skip this section because of its unusual title, as I believe it is perhaps the most important aspect of effective goal setting. The concept of be→have→do demonstrates why most individuals never achieve a majority of his or her goals.

When operating on automatic, humans tend to live based on a simple premise of do→be→have. In other words, "if I *do* this, then I will *be* that, and therefore, I will *have* this." A typical example:

> If I *do* save lots of money, then I will *be* wealthy, and therefore, I will *have* financial security.

The typical person, on an average day and at the subconscious level, is inclined to set goals based on the do→be→have state of being. On the other hand, successful goal setters do not operate his or her life from the premise of favoring action above all else without first believing in the objective at hand and taking ownership of it.

One may argue that most individuals do not function from a place of ownership first and thus set goals based on what he or she needs to do. As a result, many have trouble achieving the desired outcome of what he or she hopes to be or wants to have.

I submit the successful goal setter functions in the rare conscious state of be→have→do. Take a look at how a mere reshuffle of priorities may result in dream achievement never thought possible:

> If I *be* (am) someone worthy of wealth, I will *have* a sense of financial security; and therefore, I will *do* what is necessary to earn and save more money.

By moving toward favorable action, the prudent goal setter has first decided he or she is a person worthy of the wealth and the financial security it brings, thus creating a built-in motivation to earn more and save more.

Here is another typical example of the less successful do→be→have approach to problem solving:

> If I do this popular diet, I will be twenty-five pounds lighter; and therefore, I will have a thinner body.

Now look at the subtle, yet more successful be→have→do affirmation approach to the same goal:

> I will be a thinner person because I have the courage to do what is necessary to lose twenty-five pounds in a healthful way.

Again, the decision is made first to assert a state of being as a thinner person. Next, have the courage to believe in the goal through continued affirmation. Then, do what is necessary and ethical to succeed.

The concept of be→have→do is counterintuitive, although geared to the anticipated result of saving money, losing weight, or whatever the personal or professional goal. More often, individuals operate on a subconscious level influenced by a well-intended upbringing or external influences. Each focuses on the action of doing before deciding he or she is conscious of being—and worthy of having—what is important.

Such a conscientious approach to living, in general, and goal setting, specifically, is unconventional. That is why it works. If conventional wisdom always worked in life, a majority of individuals would be successful in both personal and professional pursuits, thus rendering self-improvement books and seminars to extinction.

The ubiquitous 80/20 Rule is another example of conventional wisdom versus counterintuitive decision making. Here, the approximated twenty percent minority prevails by prescribing to an unconventional method, i.e., be→have→do; that if implemented on a consistent basis, works a theoretical eighty percent of the time, or more often than not. The approximated eighty percent of individuals practicing conventional wisdom in goal setting, i.e., do→be→have, succeed about twenty percent of the time, or at least less often than those practicing be→have→do.

To be sure, the 80/20 rule is not scientific, although I challenge any reader to begin observing those around you at work, at home, and in public. You may find the minority, or the perceived twenty percent, is receiving a majority, or the perceived eighty percent, of what each is seeking in his or her life. The other eighty percent, more or less, is clamoring over the remaining twenty percent, or thereabouts, of the personal and professional achievement pie.

By embracing the be→have→do concept, you are using the power of affirmation first to be who you want to be; next, have what you want to have; and then, do what is necessary to bring your goal to completion. In other words, successful action follows those who first decide each deserves what he or she wants to achieve.

* * *

An important first step in effective goal setting is to set targets that are believable and achievable. Next, write down your plan, and work the plan. Remember to give the plan a K.I.S.S. by keeping it super simple; and S.M.A.R.T., as in specific, measurable, attainable, realistic, and time-bound.

Practice the cognitive art of be→have→do by first making the personal decision of being worthy of your goals. Next, take ownership of having what is important to you, your loved ones, and colleagues. Then, do what is necessary—in an ethical and caring way—to bring your goals to fruition.

It is sometimes said that individuals do not change, although everyone does have the ability to transform. I challenge you to be transformational in your goal setting. Begin with the destination in mind, remembering to enjoy the journey, as the ride may be the best part of achieving your goals and dreams within the Ten Domains.

PART II

THE TEN DOMAINS

The Ten Domains play a significant role in setting objectives for an overall happy and productive life. It is important to understand that each domain is optional, based on individual preferences, and may be added or subtracted as appropriate.

Keep in mind that the Ten Domains, presented here in generic form, may be expanded or contracted to suit the personal and professional values and beliefs of the goal setter. Individual lives are unique, fluid experiences, not one size fits all mantras. The Ten Domains are no exception. Therefore, I encourage readers to think of personal needs and wants when studying each domain. To borrow from an old cliché, "take what you need, and leave the rest."

I also urge readers to redefine each domain, if necessary, until you are comfortable with how it supports the goals and dreams that are the heart of your current circumstances at home, in the workplace, and beyond.

Five

Exploring the Ten Domains

L et's take a dive into each of The Ten Domains of Effective Goal Setting.

1. Spirituality

Whether religious, spiritual, or neither, the first domain, *Spirituality*, is an opportunity to explore what is important to you in your convictions or beliefs. What is your purpose? What defines your faith? Who is your higher power, and what role does that entity play in your life? What are the values by which you live? Spirituality is perhaps the most personal of the domains and therefore leads the list.

For some, Spirituality drives the other domains. For others, it is not included in his or her goal setting. Another reminder that using the Ten Domains as a goal setting template is negotiable. It is more a framework and less a rigid stencil.

In the Spirituality domain, short term goals such as plans for the upcoming year may include the desire to attend church, temple, or mosque more often. Long term goals, such as three, five, or ten-year plans, may encompass bucket list items such as reading the Bible or Quaran from cover to cover or remembering to pray—or keep the faith—during life's more challenging moments.

Nevertheless, think of both short term and long term intentions that are relevant to your spirituality, religious beliefs, or personal values on your journey of life here on Earth.

2. Family

The next domain, *Family*, provides an excellent opportunity to reflect on your interactions with those closest to you by birth or marriage, including spouse, partner, significant other, children, grandchildren, siblings, parents, in-laws, and perhaps your pets.

Family is the ideal domain for writing down your thoughts and feelings about loved ones most important in your life. Place personal aspirations that are approachable on this year's wish list, and set more challenging hopes and desires in a broader timeline.

The Family domain is perhaps the most compelling of the ten, more about love and devotion and less about a bulleted list of objectives. Tread with care, and be passionate. I have both observed and experienced that when the dust settles following heartbreaks, such as the death of a loved one, divorce or breakup, job loss, financial stress, and so forth, it is family members that are standing beside us in times of need.

Remember to embrace those offers of genuine love and devotion and find opportunities to return the affection in ways that you are comfortable.

3. Health

Any goal setting exercise that includes long-term ambitions perhaps needs a domain about prolonging one's life—as much as it is controllable—to have a reasonable opportunity to stay awhile and enjoy what is important to us.

There is a time of year when advertising is inundated with weight loss and exercise programs, echoing the enormous market for health and wellness. The desire for improved health is a beneficial obsession. But fads aside, the *Health* domain represents an excellent opportunity to set reasonable targets for the year—and beyond—regarding your body, mind, and overall well-being.

One of my favorite anecdotes is from the 1999 Brad Pitt movie. *Fight Club*,[1] adapted from the Chuck Palahniuk novel of the same title; and celebrated as a refrain by the contrarian financial website, *Zero Hedge*:

> *On a long enough timeline, the survival rate for everyone drops to zero.*

Since we are living in a humble reality that is impossible to overcome, we may as well do whatever is necessary to extend our inevitable and finite timeline here on Earth. The Health domain provides the opportunity to stretch the inescapable.

One may argue that Health is worthy of being the number two domain, after Spirituality, as we cannot take typical achievements from the other domains to any promised land. Thus, be wise by maintaining your health from head to toe.

Your loved ones and workplace partners are depending on you.

* * *

[1] *Fight Club,* directed by David Fincher (Century City, CA: 20th Century Studios, 1999). Based on the novel by Chuck Palahniuk, *Fight Club* (New York: W.W. Norton & Co., 1996).

4. Education

One may label the *Education* domain as personal and professional development. Lifelong learning has become paramount to success in both professional and personal pursuits. How are you meeting the continuing education requirements of your profession or occupation in the next qualifying year? What are your long-term goals regarding first or advanced college degree attainment?

Nonprofessional training activities should be included in the Education domain as well, if appropriate. Personal interests may include obtaining a private pilot's license, improving your golf game beyond a good walk spoiled, learning to play bridge online, taking a beginner's yoga course, or attending a self-improvement seminar, as I did when first exposed to the powerful Ten Domains method of goal setting.

A critical component of the Education domain is the quest for learning should be an ongoing practice in life. The Greek philosopher, Solon, perhaps said it best:

" Grow older learning something new every day. "

5. Career

We may forever debate how skill, ambition, personality, and luck influence career success. Just as important is how each of us defines the personal measurements of success. Money as a yardstick? Making a difference? Providing for loved ones? Excellent benefits package? Contributing as part of a team? Being on a mission of purpose? Perhaps all of the above, and more?

Nevertheless, the *Career* domain provides a footprint to think about what is important to you from an activity we perhaps spend half of our waking life pursuing.

In today's dog eat dog world of work, some employees and business owners are reexamining the time and energy invested in the workplace relating to the return on investment of income and self-fulfillment. He or she may feel held hostage from the pursuit of a work/life balance. Other workers are content, whereas the career-centered may consider his or her occupation as the defining aspect of life. This level of career commitment is evident in a typical *New York Times* obituary, where professional achievements often dominate the headline.

Find your common ground by using the Career domain to establish a clear perspective of what is important to you in your professional life and how it affects all other areas of your being.

Here is the doctrine I follow within the Career domain of life:

> Discover what you enjoy; then make every effort to be the best in the world at it, thus allowing you the opportunity to make a living doing it.

Whether an employee, business owner, volunteer or homemaker—perhaps all four—or seeking employment, the Career domain provides an excellent opportunity to write down what you believe is your professional mission, now and in the future. For twenty-five years running, mine is

" *Making a living by making a difference.* "

What is your career mission statement? Keep it simple, make it smart, and write it down.

6. Money

Did you know that everyone earns the same amount of money? I call it:

" *Not enough.* "

Money is another domain that is more personal in nature. However, it is wise to leave emotions out of our money management and set goals with purpose.

Ask for a raise this year? Invest more, or more often? Hire

a financial advisor? Build an emergency fund? Refinance a mortgage with a lower interest rate? Improve your credit rating? Construct a workable budget? We all know the possibilities for financial improvement are endless.

Pick and choose what is important to you in the near term, such as eliminating a credit card balance and reach farther out for higher aspirations such as paying off that onerous student loan. Treat personal financial management as a business, and you are more apt to prevail.

As far as making more of it? Consider the principle in the Career domain of first doing what you enjoy and then being the best possible at your chosen occupation. The money may follow your passion.

7. Social

The *Social* domain could be part of the Family domain, although it is listed as a separate area to reflect what is important to you when away from your family or in need of an occasional break from loved ones. Healthy and open social connections outside of the home or workplace may add joy toward keeping your life more balanced and diverse.

In addition to cultivating friendships, the Social domain may include regular attendance at your high school reunions, responsible visits to your local bar or pub, participating in social networks such as Facebook, Twitter, Pinterest, or Instagram; or more traditional social clubs such as Rotary International, your local VFW, Elks, bridge, book, women's meet up, weekend motorcycle, or vintage car group.

I have read various studies that attribute longer life expectancies to those who maintain social relationships throughout their life. I am not sure how the phenomenon of social media affects life expectancy, although rest assured, those studies are forthcoming.

Best friends and close acquaintances can bring joy to our lives. Social relationships may also lead to disappointment and heartache. Be astute in your choices, and give as much, if not more, than you take. The Social domain provides another excellent opportunity to write down your thoughts and hopes for lifelong relationships that are healthy, productive, and fun.

8. Leisure

In today's rushed world, work/life balance continues as a hot topic. I submit that individuals have the ultimate control over balancing their professional and personal domains. We may blame our boss, employer, or financial burdens for generating too much work and not enough play, although we must take responsibility for the final decision on how to best use our most limited resource: time.

The domain of *Leisure* is a fabulous place to set short and long-term goals toward spending more time doing things you enjoy, whether it is traveling, video gaming, following your favorite sports, fishing, antique shopping, reading, skiing, or hiking a nature trail. One may argue that the list of potential leisure activities far exceeds what we accomplish at our jobs.

There is no excuse for neglecting to design a plan of work/ life balance if that is important to you. The Leisure domain is the ideal place to set a life of equilibrium. I have accentuated travel as an essential component in my plan's Leisure domain. A lifelong goal that I share with my wife, Suzan, is to see as much of the world as possible before leaving it. Another reminder of the flexibility in adjusting the domains to fit your personal lifestyle, and at the same time, remain within your financial means.

The Leisure domain could be labeled as hobbies, although some goal setters maintain such a diversified list of personal interests that they address hobbies as a subset of Leisure. Separating the two is okay as well.

Perhaps the Leisure domain is more about relaxing and de-stressing as part of a broader work/life balance, whereas hobbies sometimes require effort and commitment at levels equal to our professional life. Indeed, hobbies sometimes grow into business pursuits. Another reminder that the Ten Domains are interchangeable.

Nonetheless, write down and pursue the free time activities and hobbies that interest you. Some of life's finer moments occur in the Leisure domain.

9. Community

Karma sometimes dictates that we get what we give. For some, giving back is a fundamental domain of life's purpose. Whether volunteering for a local charity; or providing a community service by offering your time, pro bono, such as a baseball coach, Girl Scouts troop leader, or a nonprofit board member, the near and long term possibilities are endless in the *Community* domain.

Transferring your skill sets from other domains such as Career, Money, Leisure, or Spirituality, may create significant, lifelong contributions to your community, country, or the world. For those in search of ways to give back, consider completing your goal setting plan in the Community domain last. I guarantee you will find resourceful opportunities from the other nine domains that may lead to a fulfilling role of charitable service in your neighborhood or beyond.

In the challenging world of today—inhabited by the haves and have-nots—boundless opportunities exist to contribute from within the Community domain, such as a volunteer or donor to charitable organizations. The Internal Revenue Service acknowledges eligible charitable donations as deductible on your tax return, thus adding possible support to your Money domain. Consult a professional tax advisor for details.

Give and let give. Community is a great domain to set profound, achievable goals each year.

10. Projects

The final domain, *Projects*, may appear as the proverbial *other* category. However, I find it a great place to quantify important projects needing completion around the house, condominium, or apartment as well as personal interest goals, such as saving for a car, truck, or motorcycle that you admire; remodeling your kitchen; or building the storage shed you promised your grandparents.

Perhaps there is a particular project in your workplace or business that is above and beyond the scope of your Career domain, yet something you are yearning to accomplish. Write it down here.

Projects may offer a diversion from the other domains and provide regular opportunities to accomplish things that contribute to a well-balanced life, not to mention the elation of finishing what you started.

* * *

It is worth repeating that if something or someone important to you does not fit any of the other domains, create a new domain. It is appropriate to have eleven, twelve, or twenty domains if that works for your situation. Nine, or eight, is okay, too.

Regardless of how many domains encompass your life plan, write down both short-term goals, e.g., less than one year; medium-term objectives, e.g., one to two years; and long-term ambitions, e.g., three to five years, or more. As always, keep it simple and achievable. You deserve to reach your dreams, although it is okay to throw in a few stretch goals as well. Any ensuing positive momentum may take you to places never thought possible.

May you achieve all that is important to you, your loved ones, and your colleagues within the Ten Domains; or from your list of the essential personal and professional areas of life. Work the plan to earn the privilege of success because you deserve the victories that come from accomplishing your goals and dreams.

PART III

ACHIEVE YOUR DREAMS

The Ten Domains of Effective Goal Setting exemplifies one of the many templates available to guide us as we strive for excellence in our lives. I was captivated by the theory of the Ten Domains when first exposed to it at that New York seminar many years ago. I have applied it to my life ever since, achieving outcomes within each of the Ten Domains that I once believed were not possible. I renew it once a year and review it several times throughout the year, making adjustments as warranted.

The primary objectives of the Ten Domains are to create your goal setting plan in writing; keep it well-rounded to the essential personal and professional areas of your life; ensure it is S.M.A.R.T., i.e., specific, measurable, attainable, realistic, and time-bound; give your plan a K.I.S.S., i.e., keep it super simple; and work the plan every day from the conscious state of be→have→do.

To be sure, you may eliminate or add domains to the list as each applies to your life and its core values.

Regardless of the extent of your personal list of domains, the most important aspect of goal achievement is first to have a written plan. Next, work the plan by believing in yourself and having complete ownership of the goals. Then, do what is necessary—and ethical—to attain as many as possible. You may be surprised when your dreams do come true.

Six

A Life's Journey

As mentioned in the Introduction, a journey may be more rewarding than the destination itself; and becomes further amplified when considering life's final destination, any afterlife beliefs notwithstanding.

Contemplate the following list of what gives life meaning based on my personal experiences and observations. Granted, it is wide-ranging and assumes a full life expectancy.

Regardless, as someone who has lost a sibling, both parents, in-laws, and friends to earlier than expected departures—and whose wife, Suzan, has the yet incurable chronic illness of Type 1 Juvenile Diabetes and its multitude of complications—join me, by combining or consolidating where necessary, in achieving what is important to our respective lives as early as is reasonable and possible.

AGE	PRIORITY
0-12	Make Family
13-19	Make Friends

20's	Make You
30's	Make Career
40's	Make Money
50's	Make a Difference
60's	Make Retirement
70's	Make Peace
80's/90's	Make Heaven

Being someone entering my late fifties, I am reflecting on my life in the above timeline and appreciating how each decade has impacted my time here on Earth, for better or worse.

The following is what I would share with a newborn if he or she could comprehend such a conversation.

In your early years, get to know your immediate and extended family on an emotional level. Be open to positive guidance, and shun, or question, any negative behavior toward you. As a teenager, seek friends that are compatible with your personality, interests, and comfort zones. Avoid befriending anyone based on fear, hate, envy, or jealousy.

As you depart the peer pressure years of youth and enter your twenties, focus on reinventing yourself as a valuable adult contributor to the world in any of the Ten Domains that are important to you. By your thirties, if not before—later being okay, too—discover an interest or occupation you enjoy; then become so good at it, you make a living doing it.

I imagine some readers are asking, "Why wait to become financially secure—however secure is defined—why not in my twenties or thirties?" As I have expressed throughout the book, considering that our life spans are a mere drop in the bucket within the world we live in, earlier is best.

Nevertheless, I have observed that many individuals seem to reach a financial pinnacle in their early to mid-forties. The US Bureau of Labor Statistics, Consumer Expenditure Survey (www.bls.gov/cex/) confirms that American household incomes, after taxes and expenditures, tend to peak in the age range of 35 to 54.

As a fifty-something, I have decided now is the time to focus on making a difference in the lives of all the good persons that reside in my universe of domains, including family, friends, colleagues, and readers. And moving forward, I look to retire by my late sixties in a personal attempt to defy the baby boom generation's fixation on working until we drop.

And moving into my swan years of the seventies, eighties, or nineties—should I be that fortunate—may be the time to take a final inventory of my life and make peace where necessary. Heaven may wait, although my body will not. But getting there—or to wherever one is traveling at the end—with serenity is paramount, as the inevitable physical breakdown looms.

Nonetheless, on occasion, I ask myself a set of poignant, albeit hypothetical questions and encourage readers to do the same. "If I was on my hospice bed today, to whom would I reach out? What would I attempt to accomplish, any physical or mental limitations, notwithstanding? What would I cherish? Regret? What would I do over? Never do again? Perhaps attempt for the first time?"

For any reader that is now in this predicament, I offer you my heartfelt sympathy and moral support, if only from afar. For everyone else, these are the questions to be asked and acted on today. For if not now, when?

Individuals that are near a natural end of life, and able to reflect before passing, more often think about what he or she should have done as opposed to pondering any regrets. Written goals are the best vehicles for eliminating the proverbial would have, could have, and should have. The one regret, regardless if achieved, is not setting goals in the first place.

Urgency is the key to enriching our lives today as opposed to the proverbial tomorrow. Whenever you struggle planning and writing down your goals within the Ten Domains, consider using the hypothetical end-of-life questionnaire. It works almost every time.

I encourage readers to rewrite their life's journey by updating the priorities within your domains based on where you have been, are now, and where you want to be.

It goes without saying that life is precious, and in the scheme of things, a virtual blink of the eye. Having an enduring plan with personal meaning, and working that plan each day, may culminate with smiles on our faces as we face imminent mortality; any physical pain or mental anguish, notwithstanding. The alternative is anxious thoughts of uncertainty sometimes witnessed by family and friends surrounding a loved one in a hospital or hospice bed.

As echoed by any travel goals within the Leisure domain, enjoy the journey in life for all it is worth. Cherish the wonderful and infinite surprises around each bend as the ultimate destination is all but known and finite.

Seven

Be a Good Loser and a
Good Winner

At the postsecondary career training schools I ran throughout my former career, we concluded graduation ceremonies by playing a video in honor of the graduating students titled, "Words to Live By." It was a screen by screen vignette of inspirational phrases, based on H. Jackson Browne, Jr.'s classic, *Life's Little Instruction Book*,[1] and was accompanied by a moving soundtrack.

One of my favorite anecdotes among many in the video was:

> " *Be a Good Loser* "
> *{next screen}*
> *Be a Good Winner.*

We are perhaps raised to be humble in defeat and overzealous in victory. In our youth, as part of scholastic sports and other young adult activities, any similar behavior may have played out just fine. However, in adulthood, overenthusiastic winners—whether an opponent or teammate—are a frequent turnoff to those around them. The more we progress in life, the less one tolerates being upstaged or made to feel inferior.

That is why it is crucial to include within your written goal setting mission statement reminders that prompt you to take your losses in stride by learning from each one; and by winning with dignity and humbleness.

In other words, lose with grace and the determination to succeed in the end, all the while celebrating your wins by including family, friends, and colleagues that were involved in the victory. Let each loved one or teammate know that you could not have done it without his or her support or partnership. Everyone will forever be grateful for the inclusion.

We already know that being a good loser brings new friends and admirers, never thought possible. Being a good winner does the same, and more.

* * *

[1] H. Jackson Browne, Jr., *Life's Little Instruction Book* (Nashville, TN: Rutledge Hill Press, 1991.)

Eight

Pulling It All Together

My goal in writing *The Ten Domains of Effective Goal Setting* was to pass on to as many interested readers as possible what I was fortunate to learn at the self-improvement seminar. The workable goal setting template—focused on the essential areas of life—that I took away from the training on that fateful day remains a powerful personal development tool.

But equipment left in the toolbox will not repair a thing.

By putting the Ten Domains to work in my life every year since I have accomplished feats on personal and professional levels never dreamed possible. Achievements include deep faith, a happy marriage, good health, earning a management certificate from an Ivy League university, a successful career in postsecondary education, debt-free financial living, close friends and family, extensive travel both in the US and Europe, active contribution to an important charity—the Juvenile Diabetes Research Foundation (JDRF)—and the willingness to finish projects that I had already started. Plus, my lifelong ambition to be a published author, writing on topics of interest to my fellow Main Street citizens, is front and center.

Now, it is your turn to benefit from the gift of practical goal setting toward the ultimate achievement of your dreams. To pull it all together, here is a review of the essential elements of *The Ten Domains of Effective Goal Setting* to keep you moving onward and upward.

- Consider using all Ten Domains to differentiate your goals for lifelong clarity.
- Set your goals in a written plan, and then work the plan.
- Give your plan a K.I.S.S. by keeping it super simple.
- Make your plan S.M.A.R.T., i.e., specific, measurable, attainable, realistic, and time-bound.
- First, *be* whom you want to be. Next, *have* what you want to have. Then, *do* what is necessary, in an ethical manner, to fulfill your dreams.
- Enjoy life's journey in all of its wonder, as the destination is defined and finite.
- Good losers are humbled, as are good winners. Either way, learn and persevere.

EPILOGUE

Share Your Success Story

I have shared a slice of my story, including a few triumphs, struggles, and heartbreaks endured along the way. And now I encourage you, the reader, to do the same.

You are invited to write to me in confidence at tendomains@davidjwaldron.com to share how *The Ten Domains of Effective Goal Setting* influenced your plan of action to set and reach goals that are important to you, your loved ones, and trusted colleagues. Receiving your response, whether lengthy or brief, would be a great honor.

Let me know your good wins and tough losses in setting your goals using the Ten Domains as your template. Just sharing your thoughts or feedback after reading the book is also welcomed. My promise is to keep your words between you and me—unless you approve otherwise—and I will respond to as many emails as possible.

For those who prefer not to share his or her success story beyond colleagues or loved ones, consider writing yourself a letter, in narrative form, that spells out your goals and dreams within the Ten Domains. Then seal the letter, and address the envelope to you with a directive not to open for three, five, or ten years – your choice. For example:

To {Your Name.} Do not open until January 1, 2026.

It is a powerful exercise that may also remind you that goals do not always play out as expected. Nevertheless, something unexpected—and worthy—just may happen because you had a written plan that incorporated the concept of be→have→do; established your goals as specific, measurable, attainable, realistic, and time-bound; kept it super simple; and, of utmost importance, you worked the plan.

* * *

May your achievable goals and dreams come true. And whenever one does not manifest as expected— borrowing from the Spirituality domain—may you keep the faith and forever persevere.

David J. Waldron is an individual investor and the author of self-improvement books for those seeking to achieve the personal and professional goals that matter most in their life.

In addition to *The Ten Domains of Effective Goal Setting*, David has written three other nonfiction books. His latest release, *Build Wealth with Common Stocks,* was written for individual investors seeking to fund life's significant milestones. *Hire Train Monitor Motivate* offers practical career-building strategies toward improving organization, team, or individual career achievements in the hyper-competitive local and global marketplaces. *A Great Place to Learn & Earn* is David's professional memoir as a former 25-year veteran of postsecondary career education.

He is working with his wife, Suzan, on her memoir, *One of a Million Faces*, about living and coping with Type 1 diabetes and its complications.

David earned a Bachelor of Science in business studies as a Garden State Scholar at Stockton University and completed The Practice of Management Program at Brown University. He and Suzan reside in historic South Central Pennsylvania, USA.

Take control and achieve your dreams at davidjwaldron.com.